Mermaid
COLORING BOOK

MW00947908

ILLUSTRATIONS BY:

VISIT US ONLINE:
WWW.YOUNGDREAMERSPRESS.COM

TAG US ON INSTAGRAM
FOR A CHANCE TO BE FEATURED:
WWW.INSTAGRAM.COM/YOUNGDREAMERSPRESS

WE'RE ALSO ON FACEBOOK:
WWW.FACEBOOK.COM/YOUNGDREAMERSPRESS

ISBN-13: 978-1-989790-64-9

©2020 YOUNG DREAMERS PRESS
ALL RIGHTS RESERVED.

NO PART OF THIS PUBLICATION MAY BE REPRODUCED, DISTRIBUTED,
OR TRANSMITTED IN ANY FORM OR BY ANY MEANS INCLUDING
PHOTOCOPYING, RECORDING, OR OTHER ELECTRONIC OR MECHANICAL
METHODS, WITHOUT THE PRIOR WRITTEN PERMISSION OF THE
PUBLISHER, EXCEPT IN THE CASE OF BRIEF QUOTATIONS
EMBODIED IN CRITICAL REVIEWS AND CERTAIN OTHER
NON-COMMERCIAL USES PERMITTED BY COPYRIGHT LAW.

BUT WAIT, THERE'S MORE!

VISIT GO.YOUNGDREAMERSPRESS.COM/MERMAID

TO JOIN OUR NEWSLETTER AND
MAKE THEIR WORLD MORE COLORFUL WITH
FREE PRINTABLE COLORING PAGES!

ALL PAGES SIZED FOR 8.5 X 11 PAPER AND INCLUDE A WIDE RANGE OF SUBJECTS INCLUDING:
ANIMALS, KITTENS, MERMAIDS, UNICORNS, MANDALAS, AN ASTRONAUT, PLANETS,
A FIRETRUCK, A CONSTRUCTION VEHICLE, CUPCAKES, AND MORE!

978-1-989387-13-9

CHECK OUT OUR FULL LINE OF COLORING BOOKS TODAY

WWW.YOUNGDREAMERSPRESS.COM

Young DREAMERS PRESS

DREAM. INSPIRE. CREATE.

978-1-989387-46-7

978-1-989387-94-8

978-1-989387-96-2

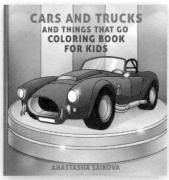

978-1-989790-09-0

978-1-989790-13-7

978-1-989790-41-0

978-1-989790-64-9

978-1-989790-93-9

978-1-989790-36-6

978-1-989387-87-0

978-1-989387-88-7

AVAILABLE FOR ORDER
AT MOST MAJOR
RETAILERS & INGRAM

THEY EVEN COME IN
MULTIPLE LANGUAGES
(FRENCH, GERMAN, ITALIAN,
SPANISH, AND A FEW SELECT
OTHERS)